PRAYERS

FOR

A Mother's Day

Compiled by

Ruth Bell Graham

THOMAS NELSON PUBLISHERS®
Nashville

A Division of Thomas Nelson, Inc.
www.ThomasNelson.com

Published in Nashville, Tennessee, by Thomas Nelson, Inc.

The Bible version used in this publication is THE NEW KING JAMES
VERSION. Copyright © 1979, 1980, 1982, Thomas Nelson, Inc., Publishers.

The artwork in this book is by Helen Allingham and
is used by permission of Inter Publishing Service Ltd.

Every effort has been made to contact the owners or owners' agents of copyrighted
material for permission to use their material. If copyrighted material has been
included without the correct copyright notice or without permission, due to error
or failure to locate owner/agents or otherwise, we apologize for the error and ask
that the owner or owner's agent contact Thomas Nelson and supply appropriate
information. Corrrect information will be included in any reprinting.

Library of Congress Cataloging-in-Publication Data on file

Printed in the United States of America
03 04 05 06 07 QWT 5 4 3 2

I'm not sure mothers need to be taught how to pray—

any more than they need to learn how

to talk to their husbands or their earthly fathers.

We just talk—impulsively, spontaneously, and sometimes interminably.

The lovely part is that while husbands and fathers

grow weary of interminable conversations, God delights in them.

But for those who may be inexperienced or shy,

we have collected a few thoughts to help you on your way.

A glorious, happy, interesting adventure lies ahead.

—Ruth Bell Graham—

THE EXAMPLE
OF LITTLE CHILDREN

Father, thank You that Your Son
never told the little children to be like the disciples,
but He told the disciples to become
as little children. We can learn so much from our children
(when we're not too tired to learn).

Ruth Bell Graham

An Unborn Child

Lord, I am afraid.

Anytime now this child that I am carrying will be born, and for some reason I am anxious. I fear delivery . . . the pain, the unknown. I question and worry. Will this child be all right? If not, will I be able to accept and cope? Please, Lord, help me!

Quietly, I hear You say, "Haven't I promised to gently lead those who are with young (Isa. 40:11)? Haven't I said, 'I have made and I will bear; even I will carry, and will deliver you' (Isa. 46:4)?"

Yes, Lord, You have promised. Help my unbelief.

Gigi Graham Tchividjian

A NEWBORN SON

Let our little son become a man of God, and give us
the wisdom to show him the way.
May he have a hunger for You, Lord, and Your Word.
Help him to experience the fulfillment
of knowledge and the rewards of hard work.
Let his days be filled with laughter and play, and give him
the protection of good Christian companions.
Instill in him the ingredients for healthy self-esteem
so that he has the confidence to reach for
his dreams and to reach out to others in need.
We dedicate this little one to You and ask You to give him
all the richness of a life in Christ.

Rolfina Birger

STRENGTH FOR A NEW MOTHER

Lord, as a new mother, I am often so tired.
I never seem to have a minute for myself—always something to do,
and no strength left to do it. Getting up at night with
the baby wears me out, and I tend to become impatient with everyone.
I do not like myself this way.
Please give me an extra dose of Your strength
and patience right now. And help me to get a good night's rest.

Thank You.
So He giveth His beloved sleep.

Gigi Graham Tchividjian

A NEW HOME

Dear Lord, we've prayed
and planned
and built this house,
and here we pause,
for You alone
can by Your presence hallow it
and make this house a home.

Ruth Bell Graham

A Young Child's Future

Lord, as I stand beside this crib,
watching this little boy fall asleep . . .
his blond curls sticking to his small, damp forehead,
his chubby fingers wrapped tightly around his blanket,
my heart is filled with emotion, wonder, and awe.
I have so many dreams and ambitions for him.

Please help me to remember that he is first of all Yours,
and that the most important thing of all is that he grow to love
You and follow You. So, Lord, tonight I put aside any and all
prayers that could have their roots in selfish motherly desires,
and pray these words for him,

Beloved child, be steadfast, immovable, always abounding
in the work of the Lord. (1 Cor. 15:58)

Because, Lord, if this prayer is answered, then one day I will
be able to say with John that my greatest joy is knowing that
my children are walking in the truth.

Gigi Graham Tchividjian

LOVING CHILDREN AS INDIVIDUALS

Lord, remind me each day that these precious children are
so different from each other and from me!
You created them so uniquely. Show me, as their mother,
how to love each one of them just the way
they need to be loved individually. Help me love them according
to their own personality and needs and not just
the way that comes easiest to me.
Give me discernment as I learn their needs, and creativity
as I learn to love them accordingly.

Sandra Stanley

WIFE, MOTHER, AND HOMEMAKER

Thank You, Father, that You have liberated me
to be a wife, mother, and homemaker.
I know that for some it is not possible, but for me
it is and I am grateful.
Help me never to take it for granted,
and help me to encourage others who have a choice
to realize the privilege and the joys involved,
and those who do not have a choice,
not to feel guilty.
And, Lord, somehow, make it up to them.

Ruth Bell Graham

THE MOORING POST

Little one, safe harbored now beyond
thy stormy journey into birth,
little one, wrapped warmly in the
smiles of God that brought thee to this earth.
Now tethered to the
mooring post of parents who employ
their grand and privileged
guardianship of thee—their little boy!

Lord, remind me often that parents are
intended to be a mooring post, a safe place to
stay, a sure place to cast anchor come wind
or weather. It is not the time for me to worry
about the storms beyond the bay, for now
we have the gift of a little time called childhood;
tethered to love, the little boat bobs and
weaves about the post—happy and secure!

Jill Briscoe

GOD WILL SAVE OUR CHILDREN

Father, You said that You would contend
with those who contend with me
and You will save our children (Isa. 49:25).
Television, magazines, the classroom, and now the Internet—
all are filled with "contenders."
But I am relying on Your promise.

Ruth Bell Graham

PROTECTION AND GUIDANCE

Dear Lord, thank You for each of our children.
They are so precious to us.

Watch over and protect them as they mature and
grow closer to You.

Help them to realize that You are all they need to live
a fulfilled life here on earth.

Let Your light shine through us for them to see so
that they may know that You are the truth and the way.

Thank You, Lord.

Jean A. Ziglar

PRAYING "ON THE HOOF"

Lord, forgive me that I have so little time to spend on my knees.
Raising children and running a busy house,
I have to do most of my praying "on the hoof," as it were.
But, Lord, You know my heart is kneeling.

Ruth Bell Graham

OUR CHILDREN'S FUTURE SPOUSES

Lord, You who ordained marriage in the first place,
although our children are still small,
we pray for the one each will marry one day.
Bring up their future mates to fear and obey You,
to study Your Word,
and to follow You joyfully so they will be
the mates our children need,
and the parents our grandchildren will need.

Ruth Bell Graham

For God to Be
What a Mother Can't Be

Lord, see in them what I cannot see.
Lord, bring to light what I do not know.
Lord, teach them of what I am not aware.
Lord, whisper to them what I have forgotten.
Lord, warn them of what I have omitted.
Lord, be for them what I cannot be.
Lord, love them, for You are all they need.

Linda C. Zaepfel

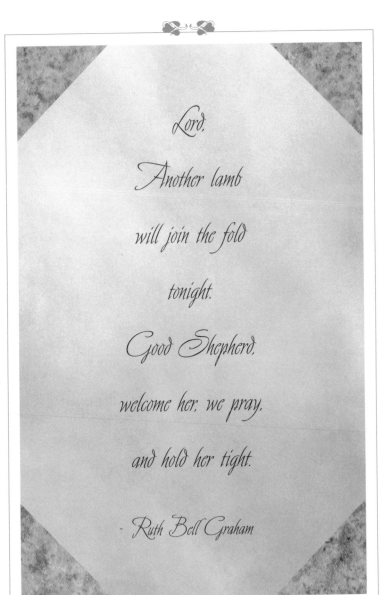

Lord,

Another lamb

will join the fold

tonight.

Good Shepherd,

welcome her, we pray,

and hold her tight.

Ruth Bell Graham

Not Making Faith
Seem Like a Burden

Lord, someone once said that anything that becomes
a burden will be discarded with relief.
So please keep me from ever giving to the children
the impression that belonging to You
and obeying You are a burden and a joyless journey.

Ruth Bell Graham

A Mother's Need
for God's Direction

Dear Lord, if I clean a floor,
I know if it is clean or dirty,
black or white,
good or bad.
But as a mother,
the answers are not so obvious.
Sometimes they are not clear at all.
My very best judgment is, at times,
shaky and confusing.
Lord, show me.
Teach me.
Be glorified through my imperfections with my children.
I love them so.
And, O Lord,
How I love You!

Ann Kiemel Anderson

A Young Boy
Away from Home

Lord, when a young boy cries
  in bed at night,
  stealthily, silently,
  never aloud.
  Newly away from family and friends,
  too old to cry,
  too proud,
  too young to know each night passes on,
  making way for a newer dawn,
  too old to stay in the nest,
  and yet too young to fly away.
  God, be near
  when a young boy cries.

Ruth Bell Graham

THE IMPORTANCE OF
A MOTHER'S TEACHING

Father, they have forbidden our children to pray in school! They no longer teach them about You or even acknowledge You. Your Word is no longer used as a guidebook. They have removed all point of reference in teaching them right from wrong.

But, Lord, don't let this frighten me. Help me to realize that it is in the home that I can instruct and teach them.

Help me to be encouraged by Samuel's mother who had him only a few short years before he went to live in the temple under the influence of Eli's wicked sons. However, he grew to be a man of God, and I like to think the early teaching from his mother had a lot to do with that.

Or Moses' mother who also had her son for only a short time before she had to give him over to the princess of Egypt to be brought up in luxury at the pagan palace. Every wish and whim was his for the asking. But because of the early teaching from his godly mother, as a grown man he chose the right path: "rather to suffer affliction with the people of God than to enjoy the passing pleasures of sin" (Heb. 11:25).

Lord, help me to be a mother like these.

Gigi Graham Tchividjian

God's Will

Lord, You know me and my child better than we know ourselves.
You know how I feel about this issue
and my desire for Your help. Lord, I give this over to You,
knowing that Your answer will be what is best.
Not my will, Lord, but Yours be done.

Peggy J. Moore

Being Satisfied
with God's Mercy

Lord, the psalmist cried,

> Oh, satisfy us early with Your mercy,
> That we may rejoice and be glad all our days! (Ps. 90:14)

And, Lord, we ask this for our children, early in life,
to know what it is to be satisfied with Your mercy.

Ruth Bell Graham

Strength for Mothers

Lord, the psalmist prayed,
"Give Your strength to Your servant" (Ps. 86:16),
and my heart echoes his prayer.
Not just spiritual strength, but plain old physical strength.
I get so tired straightening, cleaning, cooking,
that at the end of the day when
I should be the sweetest to my family, I am a grump.

Ruth Bell Graham

A MOTHER'S PRAYER

Heavenly Father, I praise and thank You for the privilege of coming before You humbly and interceding on behalf of my children.

Keep their hearts tender and sensitive to Your voice. Give them a love for Your Word and willing hearts to obey it. Help them to desire to walk before You in righteousness all the days of their lives. May they grow in the wisdom and knowledge of the Lord. Give them a heart of compassion and concern for the lost and the wounded. Lead them to a place of service in Your kingdom's work.

Lord, send a guardian angel to watch over their going out and their coming in, and lead them not into temptation, but deliver them from the evil one.

Send enough rain to keep them dependent on You but enough sun to give them hope and encouragement. And, Lord, when they're standing at the crossroads trying to decide which path to take, put a person of faith there to point them in the right direction.

Thank You for Your blessing, Your provision, and Your great love for my children. I ask this prayer in the name of the Father, the Son, and the Holy Spirit.

Shirley M. Dobson

Choosing Right

Lord, there are so many subtle temptations today.
Please help the children learn early in life
the fine line between right and wrong and make a habit
to choose the right.

Ruth Bell Graham

PROTECTION AND FRIENDSHIP

Father, please guard my children by day and by night.
Keep them in Your care. Raise up for them
friends who know You and love You;
bring them into their lives to reinforce Your ways and values.
Teach my children the value of Christian friends,
that they may seek them out.
Prepare them to be a trusted friend to others
just as You are to us.

Lori B. Whiteman

A Child Who Has Run Away

Lord, why did he run away? Was it something I did
or didn't do? Doesn't he know that I love him?
That I care? It is so hard to have him turn his back
on us. To have him far from home and family.

Lord, please place a hedge of protection about him.
Keep him from harm and from harming others as well.

It is so difficult to accept that there is little that I
can do except to continue to love. Mothers like
to fix things, make things better, and this time I can't.
Please give me patience to wait on You.

Gigi Graham Tchividjian

THE DEATH OF A FATHER

Father, please fill in the empty, hurting places
in my children's hearts where
the absence of their father continues to touch them.
Be with them in their pain.
Take away their fears and give them hope.

Lois M. Raboy

TRUSTING GOD
FOR THE IMPOSSIBLE

Father, You have helped me to see that I am to take care
of the possible where the children are concerned,
and to trust You for the impossible.
Now please help me to understand the difference.

Gigi Graham Tchividjian

QUIET

Lord, please help my children stop bickering.
It grieves my heart that they don't love each other more . . .
the way You intended them to,
the way I intended them to. So many petty differences,
so much trivial history to their arguing.
Lord, also help me.
I'm tired of running interference,
and sometimes I end up being just plain unfair.
I need quiet. I long for harmony.
Most of all I need Your wisdom.

Susan Ells

I bring my little ones to You,

commit each to

Your loving care,

then carry them away again

nor leave them there;

forgetting You

who lived to die

(and rose again)

care more than I.

Ruth Bell Graham

A Prayer for
Hurting Mothers

Be tender, Lord, we pray
with one whose child
lies dead today.

Be tender, Lord, we plead
for those with runaways
for whom moms bleed.

But be tenderest of all with each
whose child no longer cares . . .
is out of reach.

Ruth Bell Graham

SEEING THE "RED LIGHTS"

Years ago a member of the family borrowed my father's car.
About four miles from the house a red warning light lit up
the dashboard. Because the driver's personal car had a red light
that went on intermittently and without consequences, she
ignored the light. This resulted in extensive damage to my
father's vehicle. God used that circumstance to touch my spirit.
From that day I began to pray the following prayer:

Dear Lord, as my sons grow to manhood, please
give me the insight to see very clearly any serious
"red lights" in their lives and the wisdom to act quickly
and wisely to guide them at these critical times.

Helen "Dixie" Oliver

WISDOM, PEACE, AND COURAGE

Father, may wisdom, peace, and courage
be in my child's heart, and may
the Holy Spirit within him guide his words and actions.

Barbara Bush

TAKING A "JESUS BREAK"

Lord, help me to remember on days when things get out of control that there is a time to stop and think. I have so often been reminded of the words from Isaiah that seem to speak to me at times like these:

Come . . . enter your chambers,
And shut your doors behind you;
Hide yourself, as it were, for a little moment,
Until the indignation is past. (Isa. 26:20)

Before I blow it, please help me to remove myself and take a quick "Jesus Break."

Gigi Graham Tchividjian

A Prayer for a Young Boy

May he face life's problems
as he faced his broken bike when he was small,
working till he'd traced each problem to its source
and fixed it;
all was a challenge he'd accept with curiosity
and then work night and day.
What's losing sleep when interest is involved?
Hobby or problem
he never turned loose till it was solved.
When he is a man
and man-sized problems stare him in the face,
interested or not, Lord, give him grace.

Ruth Bell Graham

A VARIATION OF
EXODUS 35:31-32

Lord, fill me with skill and ability and knowledge
in all kinds of crafts so that
these children will be artistic designs of gold, silver,
and bronze fit for Your kingdom.

Ruth Graham McIntyre

ENCOURAGEMENT FOR CHILDREN

Lord, it is so easy to be negative. To focus on what has not been done—the bed left unmade, the clothes unhung, the forgotten schoolbooks—instead of the good.

It has been said that people fail because of discouragement more than anything else. Please help me to remember the words of David concerning his son Solomon:

> Prayer also will be made for Him continually,
> And daily He shall be praised. (Ps. 72:15)

Please help me to be a source of positive encouragement to my children.

Gigi Graham Tchividjian

A TROUBLED SON

Lord, I cry for wisdom to guide our troubled son.
The enemy challenges his trust in You.
Give me a heart to understand his deep distress,
a mouth to express Your grace, and arms
to show my precious child divine strength and protection.
Oh, Love, You will not let him go.
I rest my weary soul in You.
In Jesus' name. Amen.

Virginia Page Rohrer

TEENAGE CHILDREN

Father, my children have become teenagers! I feel as though I've landed in a foreign country; the rules have changed, the language is different, and the culture is difficult to understand! Gone are the days when they scrambled excitedly into my bed, asking, "What are we going to do today, Mom?" To spend time with them now requires a meeting complete with daily planners. Where did those children go who held my hand, made mud pies, and went to bed before I did?

Father, help me change to be the mother they need now. Shut my mouth when I am tempted to speak before I've listened. Open my mind to consider their ideas and interests that are different from mine. Teach my tongue to speak words of wisdom and encouragement. Lay my heart open to love them in the midst of adversity. Strengthen my faith, Lord, that the seeds of truth that have been planted in their hearts will guide them.

Most of all, thank You, Lord, for these precious children You've given me the honor to love and adore.

Kathryn Beausay

A GENTLE VOICE

Lord, please help me develop a gentle,
pleasant tone of voice.
Someone once said, "Most of the tensions of everyday life
are caused by tone of voice."
I know it's true with me. So please help me.

Ruth Bell Graham

LIFE LESSONS

Dear Father, You have privileged me to watch my girls grow and claim their own space as You have moved them through the various stages of life. Please help them to learn these things:

First, to *accept.* A lot of things in life they must just accept—such as how people are. They need to learn that they can't change another person unless the person feels the need. May they know early in adulthood that "in acceptance lieth peace."

Second, add *gratitude* along with the acceptance of people and circumstances. May they express gratitude all around—lower expectations and higher appreciation.

Third, to *focus* or *prioritize.* Help them quickly to center their life on Jesus, Your beloved Son. May He be their way, truth, and life. May their relationship with You each year be more knowing. May the Word be their main shaper. Help them to hunger for it as part of their daily diet, and feel undernourished without it. Keep them from unhealthy compulsion and make it just desire. May their "goal be God."

Fourth, help them to *relinquish.* I've found it hard to let some things go. Some dreams, rights, friends, ideas need to be "let go." Help them to relinquish and yield for their own health's sake. May they find out quickly that attempting to control everything is too much power and brings emptiness. I pray Your "all of grace" gift to them so that they will cling only to what is real and lasting.

I pray this for them also, Father. Make them great *learners.* "Learn from Me, for I am gentle and lowly in heart, and you will find rest for your souls" (Matt. 11:29). Answer this for them, I pray. Each is very creative. May their creativity be motivated by a *passion* for the work of building Your kingdom.

I love You above them, dear Father, but I do love them so deeply.

Ruth Claudette Rambo

A PRAYER FOR GROWN SONS

They are men now, Lord, my hands at last are emptied
Of the countless talks required for so long
And I am helpless quite before the problems
That grown sons face. I cannot right earth's wrongs,
Or smooth their pathways, but, dear Lord, You can.
Speak face to face as man to man.

I have no legacy at all to give them
But if my prayer be answered, it will give
Them more than any wealth the world can offer.
I pray: Christ be their comrade while they live.
Walk with them should they feel they walk alone.
And make Your presence daily, hourly known.

Companion them. I ask for nothing greater
Than this rich blessing for these precious ones.
The whole companionship of Christ, a young man,
As counselor and guide to these, my sons.
I loose their hands, having done all I could do,
And trust them, Lord, implicitly to You.

Grace Noll Crowell

BACK FROM THE PIGPEN

By faith, I can envision him returning, Lord, this prodigal child of mine—and Yours.

Please hasten this day when he'll get his belly full of what doesn't satisfy and reach out for love that comes from You—and me.

From Your vantage point, please send someone to him. Arrange a divine encounter for my son. Whatever it takes to bring him to his point of surrender, I release him to You for this moment.

In the meantime, help me to keep an "open door" attitude that will make the return easier for him. I pray You will remind him that in his family circle, his inheritance is waiting for him to return. I know You haven't forgotten we dedicated this baby to You.

I would swallow my pride and bury my "I told you so" in the sea of forgetfulness. Enable me, by the power of forgiveness, to erase his bad track record sealed in my memory.

I'll probably bother You about this same thing tomorrow, Lord. But I know today's only source of peace is to cast all my care upon You, for You care for me—and for this prodigal child.

Lee Ezell

ENCOURAGEMENT FOR MOTHERS

Lord, John Bunyan said that if
you want encouragement,
"entertain the promises." And, Lord, I am a mother,
and I need encouragement.
Help me search out Your promises,
stand on them, and be joyful.

Ruth Bell Graham

Lord,

Bless the children,

Hold them close,

Especially those

Who need You most.

Ruth Bell Graham

ON A DAUGHTER'S WEDDING DAY

Good morning, Lord, it is our daughter's wedding day!
Oh, the excitement . . . the joy . . . the details!

Thank You . . .

For the gift of our daughter. She has been a joy and delight,
and I release her to this new time in her life.

For answering my prayers for a godly husband for her.
You have answered them by bringing a wonderful, godly
young man into our lives.

I pray that Your perfect, unconditional love will be the
example for this young couple in the days ahead. Help them
to grow in their love for each other and You.

I want this day to be a perfect one for them. So I ask
Your help to remain calm, to remember all the details, and
to enjoy all that happens.

In Jesus' name. Amen.

Margaret Maxwell

GRANDCHILDREN

Dear Lord, I made many mistakes raising my child.
Now she's a mother. Forgive my errors and
heal her heart so that she can mother well my grandchildren.
Surround them with Your protecting angels.
Give them Your wisdom, energy, and love. Most of all,
bring them to that eternal life-giving commitment to Jesus Christ
that will one day reunite us all in heaven.
Amen.

Grace H. Ketterman, M.D.

TURNING CHILDREN'S CARES
OVER TO GOD

Lord, I think it is harder to turn the worries and cares of my children over to You than my own. For, through the years, as I have grown in faith, I have learned that You are merciful and kind.

Not one time have You failed me, Lord—why do I fear You will fail mine?

Ruth Bell Graham

DEALING WITH FEAR

Our family moved from a small apartment in Boston to a large house in Cleveland, Tennessee. For the first time the three children had their own bedrooms, which were scattered all over the house. My husband was traveling a great deal and I found myself overcome by irrational fears about their safety. I cried out to the Lord . . .

> *Father,* help me to trust You in all the details of my life. Please deliver me from fear, both reasonable and irrational.

The answer came, as it often does, from the Word.

> I will both lie down in peace, and sleep;
> For You alone, O LORD, make me dwell in safety.
> (Ps. 4:8)

Now, twenty years later, it is still the staff I lean on when tempted by fear.

Darlia Conn

A Son Who Is a Father

Father, I lift to You my son who is
now himself a new father.
May he walk cautiously and wisely in Your steps
as smaller feet follow him.

Carmelita Walker

HELPING CHILDREN
GLIMPSE GOD'S GLORY

Lord, I was reading Psalm 90:16, "Let Your work appear to Your servants, and Your glory to their children," and I thought, *There is a good reason for the order.* Work appeals to the mature, but it is important that our children glimpse Your glory first. That glimpse of Your glory makes whatever follows worth it all.

Even You, Lord, for the glory that was set before You, "endured the cross, despising the shame" (Heb. 12:2). Isaiah labored a lifetime and met a grisly death, but he saw Your glory first. Paul the arch persecutor became a "prisoner of Christ" but had first seen Your glory. Peter, James, John—all suffered for You as few men have, but they saw Your glory first.

As parents, we must see to it that we speak less of the problems, the heartaches, and the backaches of following You and doing Your work than we do of You and Your glory.

Ruth Bell Graham

BEING A GRANDMOTHER

Dear Lord, when I think about the blessings of parenting and grandparenting, gratitude sweeps over me. Thank You for the present joy of pouring myself into the open and ardent hearts of our five grandchildren. But even more than that, thank You for *what they teach me.* I see in them Your gracious forgetfulness toward my erring ways, Your eagerness to welcome me each time I come to You, and Your honesty that forces me to see truth as only a child can. Be free to correct me through them, Father. I'm open.

Thank You for the privilege of living near enough to simply watch them grow. I press the endless promises of Christ into their hearts today for protection and courage to face our chaotic world. Remind them, Holy Spirit, that consequences surround each choice. Bless them with the gift of laughter, unconditional love, respect for truth and others, early repentance, and treasured friends. I know, Lord, that my dreams for them don't begin to match Yours, so I rest in Your purposes. In the strong name of Jesus. Amen.

Gail MacDonald

ADOPTED CHILDREN

Lord, teach my children Your ways.
Give them hearts that are bent toward obedience.
I ask You in Your mercy and grace to
give them wisdom and knowledge and understanding
beyond their years and experience.
Fill their days with a sense of Your presence.
Let them begin to catch a vision of who they are in You.
I pray that their identity would
come not from their heritage, their circumstances,
or their father and me,
but that their identity would be found in You.

Terry Meeuwsen

A Child with Disabilities

There have been occasions for extended prayer time regarding my four children; but probably the most intense prayer for my family has been for my youngest grandchild. As a child with Down's syndrome, Steven has been the subject of many prayers similar to this:

Dear God, we thank You for this precious child You brought into our family to love and care for. I ask that You would enable him to be a quick learner, but most of all, that he would understand the love of Christ in his life. Even though he has definite disabilities, I have seen Your miraculous touch on his life. In fact, he has taught us many lessons about loving one another. I thank You that even as a preschool child, he is making great strides in his learning capabilities, and best of all, he is learning to quote Your Word.

Beverly La Haye

A Prayer for Grandchildren

Dear heavenly Father, thank You so much for
Your watchfulness over us and most of all for
Your great love and mercy. We thank You for being with
our grandchildren and for their accepting Your gift of salvation.
In these times especially we pray they will
seek and follow Your direction in their lives each day.
Help them to learn to trust You more in all decisions.
We pray they will be wise in their choice
of friends, and may they be a good influence to others.
We would not forget to think of their
future mates as they face daily decisions, whether large or small.
Thank You for loving us and Your many promises
to answer when we turn to You in faith.

Jeanette M. Cathy

TREATING CHILDREN
WITH LOVE, GRACE, AND MERCY

Lord, please help me to
remember to treat my children as You treat me . . .
with love, grace, and lots of mercy.
Help me not to nag them but to remember that
when I ask Your forgiveness . . .
You forgive without reminding me ten times of my wrongdoing.
You even choose to put it
behind You and remember no more.

Gigi Graham Tchividjian

A Mother's Urgent
Christmas Prayer

"God rest you merry, gentlemen,"
and in these pressured days
I, too, would seek to be so blessed
by Him, who still conveys
His merriment along with rest.
So I would beg, on tired knees,
"God rest me merry, please."

Ruth Bell Graham

GRANDCHILDREN
AS THEY GO TO SCHOOL

Heavenly Father, please watch over our grandchildren today as they go to school. Some of them may have a hard time with math or grammar, so help them listen and understand the material being taught.

May they look up to You for help each day and not just on test days. Help them to be honest, thoughtful of others, and diligent in their studies. Protect them from the evil one; shelter their minds from his lies. Guide them in their choice of friends.

Direct their steps so they may love You with all their hearts and want to serve You all their lives. This I pray in the precious name of Jesus.

Betty L. Wiersbe

A Clean Heart
and a Steadfast Spirit

Create in each one a clean heart, O God,
And renew a steadfast spirit within them.
(Ps. 51:10)

Ruth Bell Graham

A Grandson
Leaving for College

Dear heavenly Father, my sweet grandson is going off to college. I pray Your Spirit will go with him and he will continue to walk in Your footsteps as he has before. I command Satan, in the name of Jesus, to keep his hands off my grandson, for he is God's property and Satan has nothing in him. May Your angels surround my grandson and protect him from all evil forces that would try to destroy his life.

These things I ask in the precious name of Jesus Christ, my Savior and my grandson's.

Evelyn L. Roberts

A VARIATION OF JOHN 17

Father, more than anything I want my children and grandchildren to know You and to belong to You. Stay with them and care for them so that they will always be united to You. May they walk with You daily and desire to spend refreshing times in Your presence.

Keep them safe from the evil one. May they turn away from evil and not eat of the delicacies of sin. May they be sensitive and obedient to the promptings of the Holy Spirit concerning any sin in their lives.

Sanctify them in the truth of Your Word. I pray that their hearts would hunger and thirst for the righteousness of the Scriptures and that their will would be lost in the goodness and trustworthiness of Your way for them. May they never doubt Your love for them. I pray that they would continually be amazed by Your desire for intimacy and constantly stand in awe of Your glory. These things I ask in Christ's name. Amen.

Cynthia Heald

THE JOY OF
HUGGING A CHILD

Father, thank You for the joy of
hugging a little child.

Ruth Bell Graham

About the Author

Ruth Bell Graham

is the child of missionary parents,
wife of evangelist Billy Graham, mother of five children,
grandmother of nineteen,
and great-grandmother of thirteen (and counting).
She is the author of many books,
including *Legacy of a Pack Rat, One Wintry Night,*
and *Mothers Together*
(written with her daughter Gigi Graham Tchividjian).

About the Artist

Helen Allingham

(1848–1926)

was the foremost woman watercolorist of her time.
Widowed at a young age, Allingham
worked diligently at her art to provide for her family,
often using her three children as models.
Her scenes of country life in a simple bygone era
still delight and inspire art lovers.